Teacher's Notes
Victorian Children

Andrew Hammond

Series editor | Sue Palmer

Contents

OXFORD
UNIVERSITY PRESS

Great Clarendon Street, Oxford OX2 6DP

Oxford University Press is a department of the University of Oxford.
It furthers the University's objective of excellence in research, scholarship,
and education by publishing worldwide in

Oxford   New York

Auckland Bangkok Buenos Aires Cape Town Chennai
Dar es Salaam Delhi Hong Kong Istanbul Karachi Kolkata
Kuala Lumpur Madrid Melbourne Mexico City Mumbai Nairobi
São Paulo Shanghai Taipei Tokyo Toronto

Oxford is a registered trade mark of Oxford University Press
in the UK and in certain other countries

British Library Cataloguing in Publication Data

Data available

ISBN 0 19 834873 8

3 5 7 9 10 8 6 4 2

Typeset by Fakenham Photosetting, Fakenham, Norfolk

Printed in the UK

What is Oxford Connections?

Oxford Connections is a set of 12 cross-curricular books and related teaching materials for 7 to 11 year olds. The books will help you teach literacy through a science, geography or history-based topic. Each book provides the material to cover one unit from the QCA Schemes of Work for the National Curriculum in England and Wales, and the non-fiction literacy objectives for one whole year of the National Literacy Strategy. (You can find a grid of where the QCA and NLS objectives are covered on p 48 of these notes and on the inside back cover of the pupils' books.) The books can be used to focus primarily on literacy or on science/geography/history.

Literacy

Pupils need different literacies. As well as traditional texts with different purposes and audiences, they also need to be able to understand and write material presented in different forms such as diagrams, bullet points, notes and Internet displays, particularly when working with non-fiction.

Oxford Connections supports the development of these different literacies. It focuses particularly on reading and writing non-fiction, and will help pupils use effectively the different non-fiction text types (report, explanation, instructions, recount, discussion, persuasion).

Using these books will help pupils to focus on the two main elements which make a text type what it is:

◆ the language features used (for example, present tense for instructions, and past tense for recounts, use of commands in instructions etc.);
◆ the structure of the text (for example, chronological order, in the case of instructions or recounts).

The structure of a text can be represented as a diagram or framework, showing visually how the parts of the text fit together, which are the main points and how they are developed etc. (A very common example of this type of presentation is a timeline, which shows events which have happened in the past, as a continuum, the order of which cannot change.) In this book, we refer to material presented in this diagrammatic way as *visual* (*visual reports, visual explanations* etc.).

Pupils will learn to read and to present information visually (by using frameworks), thus developing good note-taking skills, and consolidating their understanding of how texts are structured. The visual texts in particular are accessible to those pupils who need more support. Using frameworks to plan their own writing will also help improve all pupils' planning and drafting/editing skills.

In this book, we have used icons to represent the different sorts of frameworks you can use, called *skeletons*. These are referred to in the *National Literacy Strategy Support Materials for Text Level Objectives* (DfES 0532/2001). They can be used as an aide-memoir to help pupils remember the structure of each text type. They appear on pp 6–47 to show you what text types are on the pupils' book pages.

Recount		Explanation	
Instructions		Persuasion	
Non-chronological report		Discussion	

Using *Victorian Children* to teach literacy

There are step-by-step instructions to teach pupils how to read and write the different text types on pp 18–47 (a six-page section for each text type). They follow this model:

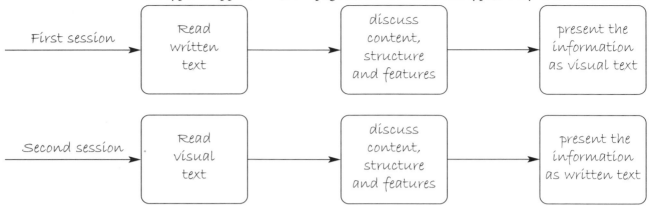

Each six-page section contains:

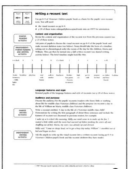

Two pages of step-by-step instructions taking you through the process described in the diagram above. They will help you analyse a written text, and then produce a visual version of that text with a group of children. You will then analyse a visual text, producing a written version.

A page describing the relevant text type.*

An example of the text type (an excerpt from *Victorian Children*) for you to read and analyse with pupils.*

The same example with language features highlighted for your reference.*

A visual version of the written text for your reference.*

can be photocopied as handouts, a poster or an OHT

There are page-by-page notes on how to use the material to cover other aspects of literacy on pp 6–17. These page-by-page notes also show how to use the material in the pupils' book for the particular subject, e.g. history.

Speaking and listening, and drama

The discussion which is inherent in this method of learning should improve pupils' speaking and listening skills. As well as helping pupils to organize and structure their ideas before writing, visual texts should prompt pupils to use the relevant language features orally, as well as in writing. Additional speaking and listening, and drama activities such as those below, can be used to further reinforce the pupils' learning.

Retelling – events can be retold by an individual or by groups taking a section from a visual recount.
Role-play – using the visuals created by the whole class to ask/answer questions in role, taking the role of the person in the recount or taking one side of the argument etc.
Mini plays – retelling an event or following an explanation visual to show how something works. Pupils could be the different parts of whatever is being explained.
Puppet plays – retelling an event or following an explanation visual.
Freeze-frame – showing sections from a recount visual or report visual. They could show different aspects of a discussion.
TV/radio reports – demonstrating knowledge using a visual report as a TV/radio report. In a TV report images could be used either pictorially or by the use of freeze framing.
TV demonstrations – following an instruction visual or explanation visual to demonstrate making something or explaining how something works.
TV/radio interviews – retelling events in recounts or using report visuals while interviewing another pupil/pupils in role.
TV/radio adverts – using a persuasive visual to make adverts.
Illustrated talks – using the visual as a prompt.
Hot seat – answering questions in role – either as a persuasion, report or recount.
Debates – using discussion visuals to have debates between individuals or groups.

Using *Victorian Children* to teach history

Victorian Children contains all the material you need to cover this topic, and to achieve the objectives of the *QCA Scheme of Work for the National Curriculum* History Units 11 and 12 (recommended for Year 5 pupils). There are page-by-page notes on how to use the material for history on pp 6–17. You can find a grid showing how the QCA objectives are covered on p 48 of these notes, and on the inside back cover of *Victorian Children* pupils' book.

Which year group should I use *Victorian Children* with?

Victorian Children has been written for Year 5 pupils (9–10 year olds). However, if your school places the topic in another year group, the history material contained in *Victorian Children* will still be suitable for use with other age groups. Although all of the non-fiction literacy objectives for Year 5 are covered, many of the objectives for other year groups are also supported. Most of the six non-fiction text types are covered in it, and language features for Years 3, 4, and 6 are highlighted in the relevant sections.

NB Throughout this introduction the term *Year 5* has been used to mean 9–10 year olds. The references in the grid on p 48 are to the *National Literacy Strategy* and to the *QCA Scheme of Work for the National Curriculum*. However, *Victorian Children* is suitable for use with P 6 in Scotland and in Northern Ireland, since it supports many elements of the *National Guidelines, 5–14* and *The Northern Ireland Curriculum*. The history content of *Victorian Children* does not conflict in any way with either *National Guidelines, 5–14* or *The Northern Ireland Curriculum*.

SCOTLAND
AND NORTHERN
IRELAND

History

Use these pages as advance organizers to provide pupils with an overview of the work to be conducted:

concept map – shows the main areas to be covered and the links between them

contents page – shows how this information has been organized in the book.

◆ Use the introduction as an aid for using the contents page – ask the pupils to find what is being mentioned.
◆ Return to the pages occasionally during teaching to help the pupils see how their learning and understanding is building up.
◆ Use as a revision aid, asking pupils to summarize what they know about each aspect.
◆ Use the concept map at the end of the topic to review all areas of the topic covered.

Literacy

Help pupils to recognize the similarities and differences between the concept map and contents page:

◆ they contain the same information, but they are organized differently;
◆ the concept map provides an overview of the ideas contained in the book and how they are interlinked; the contents page provides a linear guide to the way these ideas are organized;
◆ they both give page numbers for ease of reference.

Throughout your use of the book, demonstrate how to use the contents page – along with the index (see p 17 of these notes) – to access information when required.

History

Key concepts
◆ To identify Queen Victoria and place the Victorian period in a historical context.
◆ To infer information from a portrait.
◆ To consider what life was like for children in the past.

Key vocabulary
◆ *Victorian era, British Empire, reign, divided society, Reform Acts, Age of Invention, technology, industry, transport*

Suggested activities
◆ Ask the pupils to share their ideas about what Queen Victoria might have been like, from looking at her portrait.
◆ Hold a general discussion on the Victorians, asking the pupils to share any knowledge they already have on the Victorians. *What have they heard about this period? What are they expecting to find as they read this book?*
◆ Ask the pupils to read and copy the timeline into their own books, drawing their own pictures to accompany the text.

Literacy

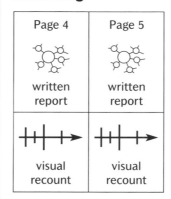

Page 4	Page 5
written report	written report
visual recount	visual recount

These pages are used as a featured example to teach the reading and writing of **report** text (see pp 30–35 of these notes).

Discuss with the pupils the process of placing events in chronological sequence. Ask them to design their own timeline, drawing on major events in their own lives or in the life of the school, and to include supporting illustrations.

History

Key concepts
- To collect information and draw conclusions about this era.
- Ways of life differed greatly across Victorian society.
- To consider how attitudes to childhood changed over time.

Key vocabulary
- *middle class, innocence, exploration, working class, workhouse, clean slates, morals*

Suggested activities
- Hold a class or group discussion on how we value childhood now. What is important to us?
- Ask the pupils to split into groups and list the important ingredients needed to make a safe and happy childhood (health, fun, opportunities, education etc.). Present their findings to the rest of the class.
- Discuss in class which of these conditions were/were not present in the lives of many Victorian children.

Literacy

Page 6	Page 7
written discussion	visual persuasion
	written discussion

Pp 6–7 feature a written discussion – this is a text which presents all sides of an issue or subject, prompting the reader to consider each viewpoint. Middle-class views on childhood are profiled against working-class views and practices.

Show the pupils how to turn the written discussion text into a visual discussion, presenting the differences between a middle-class and a working-class childhood in summary form in a grid.

History

Key concepts
- Ways of life differed greatly across Victorian society.
- There are many representations and interpretations of Victorian life.

Key vocabulary
- *daily routine, privileged childhood, nanny*

Suggested activities
- Read these pages in conjunction with pp 18–19 of the pupils' book. Ask the pupils to comment on the differences between a day in the life of a working-class and a middle-class Victorian child.
- Use hot seating to explore how the Victorian children would feel about their daily routines. Use role-play sessions to pair up a working-class and middle-class child in conversation. What would they say to each other?

Literacy

Page 8	Page 9
visual recount	visual recount

These pages are used as a featured example to teach the reading and writing of visual **recounts** (see pp 18–23 of these notes).

Ask the pupils to construct a similar visual recount for a typical day in their own lives. (link with ICT – constructing text boxes, using columns, sequencing).

History

Key concept
◆ To consider how attitudes to children and childhood have changed.

Key vocabulary
◆ *tumbling acrobats, zoetropes, flicker books*

Suggested activities
◆ Discuss the different ways in which the pupils spend their leisure time today. Ask the pupils, in groups, to list the various hobbies and pursuits they may have and present their findings to the class. Compare these with the activities available to the Victorians.
◆ Using the materials listed on pp 10–11 of the pupils' book (which should be in plentiful supply in the school stock cupboard!), construct flicker books and clowns in class.

Literacy

Page 10	Page 11
○▸○▸○▸	○▸○▸○▸
written instructions	visual instructions

Draw the pupils' attention to the layout and content of the instructions, making particular reference to:

◆ the imperative form of verbs (placed at the beginning of each sentence and used as a command);
◆ the importance of chronological sequence (following instructions in order).

History

Key concepts
◆ To infer information from a portrait.
◆ To recall information about the life of children in Victorian times.

Key vocabulary
◆ *breeched, knee breeches, modest, smart, formal style, Little Lord Fauntleroy*

Suggested activities
◆ Use to prompt a lively discussion on children's fashion in Victorian times. Would the pupils have enjoyed wearing these clothes?
◆ Ask the pupils to research fashions in the Victorian era and collect other visual examples of children's clothes.
◆ Encourage the pupils to design their own Victorian outfits in the style of the clothes in the portraits, and then to design a contemporary outfit, for a modern child. (Link with art and D&T.)

Literacy

Page 12	Page 13
⬡	⬡
written report	written report

The written text featured here can be reconstructed as a visual report. Ask the pupils to retell the information using annotated diagrams of the clothing outfits.

The photographs are a rich source of ideas for creative writing. Encourage the pupils to write poems, stories, and diary extracts inspired by the characters in the photographs. The *first* and *third person* narrative can be explored as they write 'in role' as one of the Victorian children, or use them as central characters in their stories.

History

Key concept
◆ Ways of life differed greatly across Victorian society.

Key vocabulary
◆ *drawing room, scullery, bowl and pitcher, tin and enamel baths*

Suggested activities
◆ Use these pages to show what a middle-class house might have looked like. Make particular reference to the *scullery*, a term which is less common today. Emphasize the use of decoration and period features, which are highly sought after today. (Link with Victorian legacies, pp 44–45.)
◆ Contrast this house with the type of accommodation available to poorer families (see Housing for the poor, p 22).

Literacy

Page 14	Page 15
visual report	visual report

The visual text featured here can be turned into a written report. Ask the pupils to rewrite this article without diagrams but beginning each paragraph with a new room and describing what this room was used for etc.

Refer to the use of annotations in this visual report. Discuss the need for concise notes and the use of short phrases, colons, and hyphens when writing labels.

Ask the pupils to construct a similar visual report of the layout of their own houses or the school. Indicate the importance of using annotations to show the name and purpose of each room.

History

Key concepts
◆ To compare modern and Victorian schooling.
◆ To communicate through drama their understanding of the nature of school life in Victorian times.

Key vocabulary
◆ *dame schools, ragged schools, nannies, governess, social graces, pupil teachers, the Three R's, dunce, arm band and cap*

Suggested activities
◆ Encourage the pupils to compare and contrast a day in the life of a Victorian pupil and a typical day at school for them. Write visual reports for each (use the school's timetable as an example).
◆ There are ample opportunities here for teacher-led role-play. Creating a mock Victorian classroom can strengthen historical understanding for the pupils, enhance empathy and inspire high-quality creative writing projects.

Literacy

Page 16	Page 17
written report	written report

Represent the information here in visual form (see activities for history, above).

With the factual evidence before them, ask the pupils to imagine life as a Victorian child and create a piece of prose entitled 'The Dunce'.

These pages provide a good example of a written report. Ask the pupils to write their own report, in the same style, describing life in schools today.

Pages 18–19

History

Key concepts
◆ Ways of life differed greatly across Victorian society.
◆ To recall information about the life of children in Victorian times.

Key vocabulary
◆ *journal, piece-worker, workhouse, shilling (s), penny (d), phossy jaw, canaries, phosphorous*

Suggested activities
◆ Use as the focus of a sympathetic discussion on childhood labour, e.g. *was it morally sound?* Elicit pupils' responses, e.g. *how would they feel in the girl's place?*
◆ Discuss the references to shillings, pennies, and pounds.
◆ Contrast this with evidence found in Life for the middle classes, pp 8–9.
◆ The written recount featured could be used as an effective stimulus for some lively hot-seating as the pupils pretend to be the young girl and her friends.

Literacy

Page 18	Page 19
┼┼│┼→	┼┼│┼→
written recount	written recount

These pages are used as a featured example to teach the reading and writing of **recount** text (see pp 18–23 of these teacher's notes).

Notice the informal language adopted in this style of journal, creating a very personal and honest account. Discuss the notion of audience and purpose: ask, *Who might this be intended for?*

Ask the pupils to write a poem about the poor factory girl.

Use as a resource for teaching *direct* and *reported speech*.

Pages 20–21

History

Key concept
◆ Ways of life differed greatly across Victorian society.

Key vocabulary
◆ *survey, spinning factory, reformers, dangerous conditions, poor ventilation, disease, dusty atmosphere*

Suggested activity
◆ Using the interviews on pp 20–21 of the pupils' book as reference points, hold mock interviews in class. Each child should have an opportunity to take on one of the following roles:
  – a doctor conducting a survey of factory conditions;
  – a factory manager;
  – a young factory worker.

Literacy

Page 20	Page 21
✳✳│✳ ✳✳│✳ ✳✳│✳	✳✳│✳ ✳✳│✳ ✳✳│✳
visual discussion	visual discussion

The interviews featured here should prompt a lively discussion on the controversial issue of child labour during the Victorian era. Although these pages are used to illustrate discussion text, the emotive nature of the topic can inspire a range of persuasive writing texts, including letters of complaint and speeches.

History

Key concept
◆ Ways of life differed greatly across Victorian society.

Key vocabulary
◆ *slums, tenements, back-to-back, workhouses, inmates, open sewers, contaminated water*

Suggested activities
◆ Provide the pupils with a range of resources, including excerpts from Leon Garfield's *Smith* or Dickens' *Oliver Twist*, and encourage them to build up a picture of what home life must have been like for the poor in Victorian times.
◆ Ask the pupils to prepare and perform a scene that features a group of poor children in conversation.
◆ Chair a discussion on the possible links between crime and poverty in Victorian times.

Literacy

Page 22	Page 23
visual report	visual report

These pages are used as a featured example to teach the reading and writing of visual **report** text (see pp 30–35 of these notes).

Discuss with the pupils the different styles of language used on pp 14–15 (Housing) and pp 22–23 (Housing for the poor). Highlight the formal, factual report on pp 14–15 compared with the more emotive and persuasive tone on pp 22–23, featuring phrases like '*terrible housing with dreadful conditions*' and '*dark, dirty and overcrowded*'.

Such a report could be used to inspire a piece of descriptive prose, entitled 'The Slums'.

History

Key concept
◆ There are many representations of the Victorian period.

Key vocabulary
◆ *underworld, underclasses, social reformers, Reformatory Schools, hulks, treadmills, hard labour, innocent, juvenile crime*

Suggested activity
◆ Hold a debate in class using one of the following motions:
  – *This House believes that sentencing criminals to hard labour helps to reform them;*
  – *This House believes that it is extreme poverty that drives most people to crime – the poor should be helped not punished;*
  – *This House believes that the death penalty is barbaric and should be abolished.*

Literacy

Page 24	Page 25
written report	written report

The featured written report text can be turned into a visual report (see pp 30–35 of these notes for example).

Ask the pupils to write 'in role' as juvenile criminals, sent to prison with adults. Write a letter or a diary excerpt, describing the conditions in the prison and showing either remorse or anger.

These pages are concerned with an aspect of Victorian society which has inspired many novels and plays over the years, including Dickens' *Oliver Twist* and, more recently, *Smith* by Leon Garfield. Ask the pupils to explain why this era is so romantic and emotive.

History

Key concept
◆ Ways of life differed greatly across Victorian society.

Key vocabulary
◆ *sewage systems, water supplies, sanitation, disease, cholera, typhoid, 'Great Stink', antiseptics, sterilize*

Suggested activities
◆ Research water systems and find out where your local water supply comes from. Ask the pupils to collect information from home/school/Internet on how we receive clean water today. (Link with geography/ science.)
◆ Discuss the harmful effects of using contaminated water. Discuss the reasons why there are many people in the world today who are forced to drink contaminated water. Provide the pupils with evidence of poverty and disease in today's world.
◆ Encourage the pupils to recognize how we often take things such as a clean water supply for granted, although this luxury is a recent phenomenon. Widen the discussion to consider how many other amenities we may take for granted in our lives today.

Literacy

Page 26	Page 27
༼–◯–༽	༼–◯–༽
written explanation	written explanation
	*≶ *≶ *≶ written persuasion

These pages are used as a featured example to teach the reading and writing of **persuasion** text (see pp 42–47 of these notes).

Tell the pupils they are reporters for a local newspaper in Victorian times. They have visited Narrow Street and must write a piece highlighting the plight of the residents in this area, focusing on the lack of clean water, the open sewers, and the resulting spread of disease.

History

Key concepts
◆ The work of individuals can change aspects of society.
◆ To find out about important figures in Victorian times.
◆ To present their findings in different ways.

Key vocabulary
◆ *10 Hour Act, Factory Act, sewage and water systems, mains drainage, Barnado Homes, orphaned children, suffragette, Salvation Army*

Suggested activities
◆ Ask the pupils to construct their own recount skeleton onto which they may place the important figures featured, plus any other people they can find who helped to shape Victorian life. Use a range of other resources including books, the Internet, and magazines.
◆ Ask the pupils to divide into pairs. Each pair must choose an important figure and prepare a presentation for the class which gives a synopsis of their life and work.
◆ Use hot-seating to explore the thoughts and feelings of the people featured. The pupils may take turns in pretending to be a famous Victorian reformer.

Literacy

Page 28	Page 29
┤┼┼→	┤┼┼→
visual recount	written recount

Use to demonstrate the features of recount texts, including chronological sequence and making brief, abbreviated notes.

Use the piece on Annie Besant to illustrate how to write brief biographies in chronological form. Compare and contrast this visual recount with the written recount on William Booth. Look at the different layouts, notes, and sentence structures.

History

Key concept
◆ To collect information from a range of sources and draw conclusions about the Victorian period.

Key vocabulary
◆ *Mrs Beeton's Book of Household Management*
◆ read the excerpt and discuss any difficult words and phrases.

Suggested activities
◆ Ask the pupils to design a modern-day cover for Mrs Beeton's cookery book (link with art and D&T). Discuss the following features:
  – eye-catching title;
  – relevant, supporting illustrations;
  – synopsis of book;
  – brief biography of author.
◆ Encourage the pupils to recognize that Mrs Beeton inspired many cookery books, magazines, and television programmes today. Ask the pupils to list as many cookery and home improvement television programmes as they can.

Literacy

Page 30	Page 31
written report	written report
	visual persuasion

These pages are used as a featured example to teach the reading and writing of **persuasion** text (see pp 42–47 of these notes).

Note the style of writing in the excerpt from Mrs Beeton's book. Discuss the formal language used (long, complex sentences and elaborate vocabulary). How does this compare with modern DIY articles and books? Ask the pupils to bring some into school and to compare styles, content, and visual impact.

History

Key concept
◆ To collect information from a range of sources and draw conclusions about the Victorian period.

Key vocabulary
◆ *recipes, freezing, ingredients, quarts*

Suggested activity
◆ Using modern cookery books, ask the pupils to write out a current recipe for ice-cream. Compare and contrast them with the Victorian recipes. Focus on the following:
  – vocabulary;
  – language style – formal/informal;
  – ingredients (link with science);
  – measurements and quantities (link with mathematics).

Literacy

Page 32	Page 33
written instruction	visual instruction

These pages are used as a featured example to teach the reading and writing of **instruction** text (see pp 24–29 of these notes).

Ask the pupils to plan, write, and perform a script from a 'daytime TV show' in which a resident cookery expert shows viewers how to make ice-cream. The hosts of the show will 'help' in the kitchen – and should also taste the end product.

History

Key concepts
◆ To describe the attitudes of different people to the building of a railway in the locality.
◆ To communicate their understanding of the benefits and disadvantages of railways.
◆ To identify characteristic features of Victorian transport and industry.

Key vocabulary
◆ *suburbs, viaducts, cuttings, tunnels, embankments*

Suggested activities
◆ Give the pupils role cards which give a name, occupation, and a point of view about the building of a railway in their local town (e.g. a local resident who could lose his/her home; a coach driver who would lose business; a local manufacturer who would benefit from the transport opportunities; a railway 'navvy' who would gain a job).
◆ Set up the classroom as the local 'town hall' in which you will hold a meeting between all interested parties to debate the new railway project. (Link with speaking and listening, and geography.)

Literacy

Page 34	Page 35
✳㇏ ✳㇏ ✳㇏ written persuasion	⊢⊢⊢→ written recount

The written persuasion texts provide an ideal stimulus for designing visual persuasion texts, or banners, to protest against or support the building of the railways. Encourage the pupils to make their own placards, keeping the following in mind:

◆ audience – people who may disagree with your viewpoint and need persuading;
◆ clarity of message – concise and direct slogans;
◆ language – emotive and persuasive vocabulary.

(Link with art and D&T.)

History

Key concepts
◆ To describe the attitudes of different people to the building of a railway in the locality.
◆ To communicate their understanding of the benefits and disadvantages of railways.
◆ To identify characteristic features of Victorian transport and industry.

Key vocabulary
◆ *locomotive, steam, pistons, cylinders, cranks, Brunel, London Underground*

Suggested activities
◆ Use the text to prompt a research project, looking at how the steam engine advanced industry and transport in Britain.
◆ Discuss the wider implications of the improvements in transport during the Victorian era, i.e. quicker deliveries, greater capacity, faster output, increases in imports/exports, prosperity, and reform.
◆ Ask the pupils to consider the railways today: *How are they managed? How many different companies and lines can they think of? What would life be like without the railways?*

Literacy

Page 36	Page 37
⚲→⚲→⚲ visual explanation	⊢⊢⊢→ visual recount

These pages are used as a featured example to teach the reading and writing of **explanation** text (see pp 36–41 of these notes).

Research and write up a short biography of Brunel, chronicling his many contributions to industry, transport, and design in this country.

History

Key concepts
◆ To collect information from a range of sources and draw conclusions about the Victorian period.
◆ To understand that the work of individuals can change aspects of society.

Key vocabulary
◆ *international communications*, *telegraph*, *Morse Code*, *telephone*, *electric signals*, *exchange*

Suggested activities
◆ Ask the pupils to research telegraphs and telephone systems, using a range of sources including encyclopedias and the Internet. The pupils may then present their findings to the class in visual and/or written presentations.
◆ Find more information on Samuel Morse and Alexander Graham Bell. Compile mini-biographies with the class.
◆ Encourage the pupils to recognize that the world of telecommunications in which we now live has its origins in the work of these great men.

Literacy

Page 38	Page 39
visual explanation	written explanation

These pages are used as a featured example to teach the reading and writing of **explanation** text (see pp 36–41 of these notes).

There is of course a plethora of books, articles and websites based on the theme of communication through the ages. Such resources could be used to stimulate a range of non-fiction studies including reading comprehension exercises, research tasks, and essay writing.

History

Key concept
◆ To collect information from a range of sources and draw conclusions about the Victorian period.

Key vocabulary
◆ *leisure time, Penny Farthing*

Suggested activities
◆ Ask the pupils to construct their own skeleton to show how they like to spend their leisure time.
◆ Draw a table in class (on the board or individually) to show leisure activities 'then and now'. A Venn diagram can be used to show common and separate interests. (Link with mathematics.)

Literacy

Page 40	Page 41
visual report	visual report

The visual report featured can be turned into a written report (see below).

Ask the pupils to plan and write a written report entitled 'Leisure Time in the Victorian Age'. Each text box in the visual report would form the basis of a new paragraph in a written report. A suggested layout might be:

◆ introduction – general statement about leisure time (rich/poor people);
◆ a day at the seaside;
◆ sports;
◆ cycling;
◆ parks;
◆ conclusion – comparing these pursuits with today's trends.

History

Key concept
◆ To collect information from a range of sources and draw conclusions about the Victorian period.

Key vocabulary
◆ *British Empire, the Colonies*

Suggested activities
◆ Use to extend pupils' knowledge of the history of the British Empire and to chair a balanced discussion on the positive and negative aspects of Britain's domination. It is important that the pupils understand that British history can be viewed and interpreted in different ways.
◆ Key words in such a discussion might be: jobs; discoveries; inventions; civilized; customs; colonization; power; greed; domination.

Literacy

Page 42	Page 43
written report	visual report
visual discussion	

The subject of the British Empire's colonization of much of the world should provoke a lively debate. Encourage the pupils to exercise their persuasive writing skills in speeches for or against colonialism.

History

Key concept
◆ To collect information from a range of sources and draw conclusions about the Victorian period.

Key vocabulary
◆ *legacies, epitaphs*

Suggested activities
◆ Use to remind the pupils that much of the Victorian era is still in evidence in the streets of Britain today. From architecture to furniture, the Victorian style is still very popular. Show the pupils, through the use of books, articles, and websites, common characteristics of a Victorian style so that they can then look for evidence of Victorian legacies as they travel to and from school.
◆ Compile a list of local Victorian legacies, from schools and houses to street lamps and post-boxes.

Literacy

Page 44	Page 45
written report	visual report

The visual report on p 45 of the pupils' book shows extensive use of captions – short phrases or sentences which serve as headings or titles for pictures. Ask the pupils to collect more pictorial evidence of the Victorian age (from magazines, postcards, the Internet) and then to write their own captions to fit each picture.

History

Key concepts

◆ To use vocabulary associated with children in Victorian times.

◆ That historical evidence is found from a number of different sources.

Suggested activity

◆ Use these pages to search for the meanings of key vocabulary to further pupils' understanding of different aspects of Victorian life. Identify words from reading that are unknown and use the **glossary** to further understanding and to clarify the information learnt.

Literacy

Use these pages to demonstrate how to locate information confidently and efficiently using a glossary.

Remind pupils of the purpose of a glossary – to explain the meaning of words or terms that are specific to the subject of the text.

Using some of the key words identified in both the text and these notes, scan the glossary to find some of the meanings. Point out that the words are in alphabetical order rather than subject order.

Use these pages to teach the pupils the purpose and function of a **bibliography**. Point out to pupils that a bibliography:

◆ collates all the references to other sources made in the text;

◆ provides a reference point for further reading;

◆ avoids the author being challenged for using someone else's work (plagiarism);

◆ is organized either by date of publication or alphabetically using the surname of the author;

◆ provides the date of publication, ISBN number (International Standard Book Number) as well as the title of the reference;

◆ contains some of the following sources: books, websites, articles, periodicals and journals.

Use the bibliography to find further details about one area of Victorian children.

Discuss how different source material is organized. Compare details provided in *Victorian Children* with material found in a different source.

History

Key concept

◆ To develop an understanding of different aspects of Victorian children.

Suggested activity

◆ Ask pupils to brainstorm areas they know about the Victorians and record on a whiteboard. Using the index as a reference, identify key areas that go together, e.g. housing of the middle classes and housing of the poor, and fit into the areas defined on their whiteboards. Show how they link to the conceptual map and contents on pp 2–3 of the pupils' book.

Literacy

Use p 48 of the pupils' book to locate information confidently and efficiently through using an index.

Remind pupils of the purpose of an index – to enable readers to find, at speed, specific information.

Use the index to find specific information. Point out the following:

◆ At times, it is quicker to use an index than the contents.

◆ An index sometimes doesn't take you to the information you want – you may have to go to a number of pages.

◆ Skimming is a more general approach than scanning. Both skills can be used to obtain information quickly but have different purposes, e.g. scanning when you want to know something specific, and skimming if you want a general overview before obtaining details or making a close read.

Teaching pupils how to read and write recount text

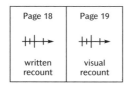

Page 18	Page 19
written recount	visual recount

Reading a recount text

Read pp 18–19 of *Victorian Children* with the pupils. You will need:

- the written recount on pp 18–19 (the text-only version on p 21 of these notes can be enlarged/photocopied/made into an OHT for annotation);
- p 20 of these notes enlarged/photocopied/made into an OHT for annotation.

SHARED READING ACTIVITY

Audience and purpose

Talk about how the intended audience and the purpose affects language and layout.

Audience – pupils in Year 5, who may have limited knowledge of the lives of the poor in Victorian times

Purpose – to chronicle a day in the life of a factory girl in Victorian times.

SHARED WRITING ACTIVITY

Content and organization

Demonstrate to the pupils how the content of this recount text is organized by showing it as a recount skeleton. Each paragraph becomes a brief phrase or sentence on the timeline, using the clock references to construct a chronological sequence (see p 23 of these notes).

SHARED READING ACTIVITY

Language features and style

Return to the text and talk about the way language has been used to achieve the effects the author intended (see annotated example on p 22 of these notes).

Note that the example chosen is a journal – a fictional recount – and as such will have the following important language features:

- written in first person narrative;
- descriptive, lively style;
- retelling events in chronological order;
- written mainly in the past tense (unless referring to continuous practices).

INDEPENDENT ACTIVITY

Working in pairs, the pupils take it in turns to answer questions about the life of a factory girl in Victorian times – as a role-play activity.

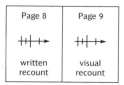

Page 8	Page 9
┼┼┼→	┼┼┼→
written recount	visual recount

Writing a recount text

Use pp 8–9 of *Victorian Children* pupils' book as a basis for the pupils' own recount texts. You will need:

- the visual recount on pp 8–9;
- p 20 of these notes enlarged/photocopied/made into an OHT for annotation.

SHARED
READING
ACTIVITY

Content and organization

Revise the content and organization of the recount text from the previous session (see p 23 of these notes).

INDEPENDENT/
PAIRED READING
AND WRITING
ACTIVITY

Ask pairs of pupils to discuss the visual recount on pp 8–9 of the pupils' book and make recount skeleton notes (see below). Notes should take the form of a timeline, setting out in chronological order the events of the day for the children, Maria and William. This can then be turned into a full written recount (see shared writing activity below). The brief timeline might look like this:

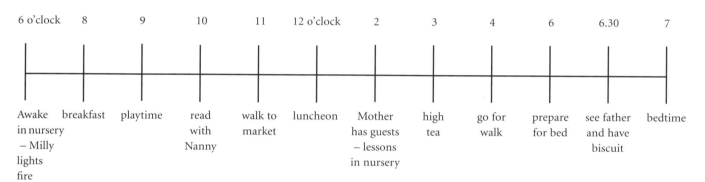

Language features and style

Remind pupils of the language features and style of recounts (see p 20 of these notes).

Audience and purpose

Discuss the audience for the pupils' recounts (readers who know little or nothing about life for middle-class Victorian children) and the purpose (to recount a day in the life of William **or** Maria, middle-class Victorian children).

SHARED
WRITING
ACTIVITY

Write a recount entitled, 'A day in the life of a Victorian middle-class child'. Demonstrate by writing the first paragraph of about three sentences and include the features of recount text discussed in previous session, for example:

I woke up at 6 o'clock this morning. Milly, our maid came in to make up the fire. I waited a little while until the room had warmed up before pushing the covers off and shuffling out of bed. Maria, my sister, was already up and dressed.

Milly said, "Come on sleepy head, we've got a busy day today, William". I stumbled out of bed and began to dress.

INDEPENDENT
WRITING
ACTIVITY

Ask the pupils to write up the visual recount into a written recount (using pp 8–9 in *Victorian Children* pupil's book and the recount skeleton they have made).

About recount text

Audience and purpose

Audience – someone who may not know much about the events.

Purpose – to retell events that actually happened.

Sometimes you may know more about the age or interests of your reader

Content and organization

- **introductory paragraph** sets the scene, so the reader has all the basic facts needed to understand the recount
- **introduction** often also hints at the main event of the recount
- events written in **chronological order** – time order
- **closing statement** – sentence(s) or paragraph to bring the recount to an end

Answer the questions who? what? when? where?

Use your introductory sentence to help you write your conclusion. If the introduction is a question then answer it in your conclusions

First this happened ... then this happened ... next ...

Language features

- written in the **past tense** because these are specific events that only happened once
- focus on **specific people, places, dates** etc.
- may be written in the **first** or **third person**
- **words and devices** to show **time order**

This usually means proper nouns, so remember the capital letters!

Stick to one or the other – don't mix them up

First ..., next ..., finally ..., In 1950 ..., Some weeks later ...

The basic skeleton for making notes is a timeline

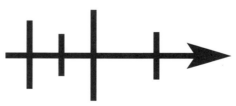

An example of a recount text

Life of the poor – a journal

Got up at 5 o'clock and set off for Bryant and May's match factory. I started work at half-past 5 sharp because it's summer (I start at 8 in winter). If a girl is late she is shut out for half the day, and loses pay – so I daren't be late! I'm what they call a piece-worker. I got 3 shillings last week. We do all right.

My sister Clarrie got me the job. She works at the factory, and earns good money, as much as 8 shillings or 9 shillings a week. Out of our earnings we pay 2 shillings for the rent of our one room.

At 9 o'clock I had my half-an-hour break for breakfast and ate a slice of bread, with a bottle of cold tea. By breakfast my feet were aching. I have to stand on my feet all day long, and they don't half swell!

At 11 o'clock we heard terrible squealing and banging. Dora's fingers had got caught in the machine and she'd only just pulled them free in time. She was fined a shilling for letting the web twist round a machine to save her fingers from being cut. The foreman said, "Take care of the machine, never mind your fingers." Girls get hurt all the time.

At half-past 1, a woman called Mrs Besant came round during our lunch break to talk to some of the girls. She says the way we work is a disgrace and she'll help us. I do hope so. But I don't want to lose my job. The Workhouse scares me even more than the phossy jaw!

Language features and style of the recount text

Life of the poor – a journal

Written in first person narrative throughout

Got up at 5 o'clock and set off for Bryant and May's match factory. I started work at half-past 5 sharp because it's summer (I start at 8 in winter). If a girl is late she is shut out for half the day, and loses pay – so I daren't be late! I'm what they call a piece-worker. I got 3 shillings last week. We do all right.

Description to develop character

My sister Clarrie got me the job. She works at the factory, and earns good money, as much as 8 shillings or 9 shillings a week. Out of our earnings we pay 2 shillings for the rent of our one room.

At 9 o'clock I had my half-an-hour break for breakfast and ate a slice of bread, with a bottle of cold tea. By breakfast my feet were aching. I have to stand on my feet all day long, and they don't half swell!

Use of past tense (when describing the events of the day – otherwise present tense for other asides and references)

At 11 o'clock we heard terrible squealing and banging. Dora's fingers had got caught in the machine and she'd only just pulled them free in time. She was fined a shilling for letting the web twist round a machine to save her fingers from being cut. The foreman said, "Take care of the machine, never mind your fingers." Girls get hurt all the time.

Focus on specific people and incidents that happened

Use of dialogue to focus on specific people

References to time throughout – to show chronological sequence

At half-past 1, a woman called Mrs Besant came round during our lunch break to talk to some of the girls. She says the way we work is a disgrace and she'll help us. I do hope so. But I don't want to lose my job. The Workhouse scares me even more than the phossy jaw!

Writer sharing own thoughts with the reader

If you are using this text with other year groups then also highlight these features:

Y3/P4
- How words can signal time sequences, e.g. **first, then, after, meanwhile**.
- Distinguishing between the 1st, 2nd and 3rd person forms of pronouns, e.g. **I, me, we, you, she, them** (e.g. **I don't want to lose my job**).

Y4/P5
- Understanding the importance of being consistent with verb tenses in recounts.
- To recognize how commas, connectives, and full stops are used to join and separate clauses.

Y6/P7
- Distinguishing between fact and opinion in personal recounts.
- To construct complex sentences using time conjunctions (**then, meanwhile**) and punctuation connectives (**colon and semi-colon**).

Content and organization of the recount text

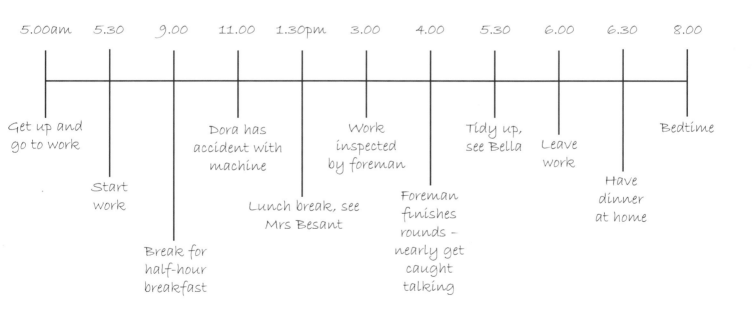

Teaching pupils how to read and write instruction text

Reading an instruction text

Page 32	Page 33
O→O→O→	O→O→O→
written instruction	visual instruction

Read pp 32–33 of *Victorian Children* pupils' book with the pupils. You will need:

◆ the written instruction text on pp 32–33 (the text-only version on p 27 of these notes can be enlarged/photocopied/made into an OHT for annotation);
◆ p 26 of these notes enlarged/photocopied/made into an OHT for annotation.

Audience and purpose

> SHARED READING ACTIVITY

Talk about how the intended audience and purpose affect language and layout.

Audience – pupils who wish to learn more about Victorian life and to create a real Victorian recipe for ice cream.

Purpose – to demonstrate how to make ice cream.

Content and organization

> SHARED WRITING ACTIVITY

Demonstrate to the pupils how the content of this instruction text is organized by showing it as an instruction skeleton (see p 29 of these notes).

Language features and style

> SHARED READING ACTIVITY

Return to the text and talk about the way the language has been used to achieve the effects the author intended (see annotated example on p 28 of these notes).

Note useful features for later use in pupils' own writing:
◆ use of the imperative form of verbs as a series of commands;
◆ a strict chronological sequence of instructions;
◆ use of connectives showing time order, e.g. *then, when.*

> INDEPENDENT ACTIVITY

In a drama session use the instruction skeleton notes as a basis for role-play. As individuals or in a group they perform a 'TV demonstration' of how to make ice cream. Make a list of useful imperative verbs that they can use in their demonstration.

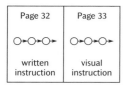

Page 32	Page 33
O→O→O	O→O→O
written instruction	visual instruction

Writing an instruction text

Use pp 32–33 of *Victorian Children* pupils' book as the basis for the pupils' own instruction texts. You will need:

◆ the visual and written instructions on pp 32–33;
◆ p 26 of these notes enlarged/photocopied/made into an OHT for annotation.

SHARED READING ACTIVITY

Content and organization

Revise the content and organization of the instruction text from the previous session (see p 29 of these notes).

INDEPENDENT/ PAIRED READING AND WRITING ACTIVITY

Language features and style

Remind pupils of the language features and style of instruction texts (see p 26 of these notes). Ask the pupils to discuss in pairs the visual instruction, *Apple Snow* on p 33 of the pupils' book.

Highlight the main differences between the written instruction on p 32 of the pupils' book for ice cream and this visual instruction. List the unique features of each in note form. The lists may take the following form:

Written Instructions	Visual Instructions
Paragraphs	Separate list of ingredients
Sentences	Numbered instructions
Connectives	Illustrations in sequence
Semicolons	Flowchart layout

It is worth mentioning to the pupils the importance of incorporating the quantities of the ingredients into the main recipe instructions (i.e. there is no separate list of ingredients at the beginning this time). Emphasize the usefulness of connectives when constructing complex sentences and showing the progression of instructions in sequence.

Audience and purpose

Discuss the audience for the visual instructions (readers who wish to make Apple Snow) and the purpose (to present an easy-to-follow recipe for Apple Snow).

SHARED WRITING ACTIVITY

Once the pupils are clear of the differences between the two versions, ask each pupil to rewrite the visual instruction for Apple Snow as a written instruction in the style of the text on p 32 of the pupils' book. Demonstrate how to write an introductory paragraph stating the intentions and describing the delicious finished product, then writing out the recipe as a full paragraph, using connectives and complex sentences, e.g.

Here is a quick and easy recipe for an old favourite, Apple Snow. A delicious dessert for dinner parties, this dish combines the sweet taste of meringues with the fresh, tangy taste of apples and lemon rind.

Begin by peeling, coring and quartering 5 green apples. Place them in a saucepan with 4 tablespoons of water and some lemon rind . . .

INDEPENDENT WRITING ACTIVITY

Ask pupils to now write the remaining paragraphs.

O→O→O→

About instruction text

Audience and purpose

Audience – someone who needs to use the instructions.

Purpose – to tell someone how to do or make something.

Sometimes you may know more about the age or interests of your reader

Content and organization

- **title** (or opening sentence) tells what is to be done or made
- **list** of what is needed
- sometimes **picture(s) or diagram(s)**
- the instructions are written as a sequence in **time order**

You will need: 2 sheets of A4 white paper, coloured pens ... etc

How to make a ...

*1. Draw a person ...
2. Cut it out ...*

Language features

- written in the **imperative,** as if the writer is talking directly to the reader telling him or her what to do
- numbers or words and devices to show the **sequence** of the steps
- all **necessary detail** included (for instance, *how many, how far, how long*)
- **factual descriptive words,** not like the descriptions in a story

*Draw a person ...
Cut it out ...*

First ... Next ... Finally ...

2 A4 sheets of white paper

NOT two lovely sheets of clean, crisp, white paper!

The basic skeleton for making notes is a flowchart

© OUP: This page may be reproduced for use solely within the purchaser's school or college

26

An example of an instruction text

Recipes

Vanilla ice cream

Dissolve half a teacup of arrowroot in a pint of milk, beat the whites of six eggs and the yolk of one and stir in, sweeten with loaf sugar, half a gallon of milk, set on the fire and let boil, then pour over the eggs and arrowroot. When cool pour in a quart of cream. Flavour with extract of vanilla; freeze.

Fruit ice cream

Half a gallon of new milk, one ounce of gelatine dissolved in cold milk and poured in, three eggs and four cups of sugar; pour in the freezer; as soon as it begins to freeze add a pound of raisins, one pint of strawberry preserves, one pound of chopped almonds, one grated cocoanut, one pound each of currants and citron; freeze.

Language features and style of the instruction text

Recipes

Title introduces what is to be achieved

Vanilla ice cream

Begin the sentence with an imperative

Dissolve half a teacup of arrowroot in a pint of milk, beat the whites of six eggs and the yolk of one and stir in, sweeten with loaf sugar, half a gallon of milk, set on the fire and let boil, then pour over the eggs and arrowroot. When cool pour in a quart of cream. Flavour with extract of vanilla; freeze.

Use of a connective to show sequence, instead of numbers

Use of the present tense

Fruit ice cream

Half a gallon of new milk, one ounce of gelatine dissolved in cold milk and poured in, three eggs and four cups of sugar; pour in the freezer; as soon as it begins to freeze add a pound of raisins, one pint of strawberry preserves, one pound of chopped almonds, one grated cocoanut, one pound each of currants and citron; freeze.

Ingredients referred to within complex sentences rather than in a list

Effective use of adverbial phrase to show when to add (verb) further ingredients

If you are using this text with other year groups then also highlight these features:

Y3/P4
- ◆ To show the end of a sentence with a full stop and the beginning of the next with a capital letter (e.g. **pour in a quart of cream. Flavour with extract . . .**)
- ◆ Using adjectives to convey taste (pupils to write an imaginary review of what the ice-creams might taste like).

Y4/P5
- ◆ To use subheadings to organize instructions (e.g. **Vanilla/Fruit ice cream**)
- ◆ Further practice in using verbs – this time using the imperative form (e.g. **Dissolve half a cup . . .**)
- ◆ Using time connectives to join clauses together and to show sequence (e.g. . . . **let boil, then pour . . .**)

Content and organization of the instruction text

Recipe for vanilla ice cream

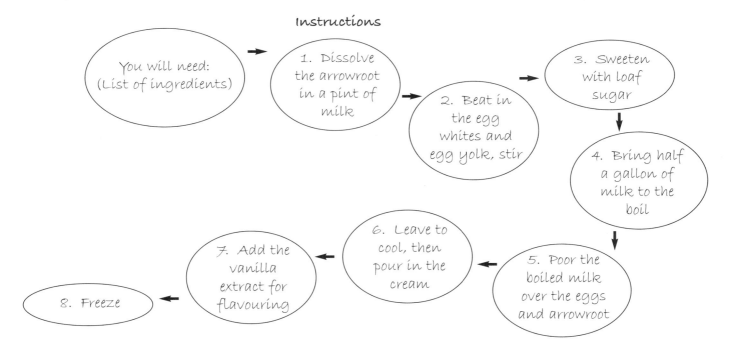

Instructions

You will need: (List of ingredients)

1. Dissolve the arrowroot in a pint of milk

2. Beat in the egg whites and egg yolk, stir

3. Sweeten with loaf sugar

4. Bring half a gallon of milk to the boil

5. Poor the boiled milk over the eggs and arrowroot

6. Leave to cool, then pour in the cream

7. Add the vanilla extract for flavouring

8. Freeze

Teaching pupils how to read and write report text

Page 4	Page 5
written report	written report

Reading a report text

Read the written report in the top half of pp 4–5 of *Victorian Children* pupils' book (not the visual report in the bottom half) with the pupils. You will need:

◆ the report text on pp 4–5 (the text-only version on p 33 of these notes can be enlarged/photocopied/made into an OHT for annotation);
◆ p 32 of these notes enlarged/photocopied/made into an OHT for annotation.

> SHARED READING ACTIVITY

Audience and purpose

Talk about how the intended audience and purpose affects language and layout.

Audience – pupils who may know little about the subject and/or have preconceived ideas and expectations of Victorian life.

Purpose – to introduce the Victorian era, chronicling the major changes and social reforms which took place during this period of British history.

> SHARED WRITING ACTIVITY

Content and organization

Demonstrate to the pupils how the content of this report text is organized by showing it as a report skeleton. Each paragraph becomes one arm of the report skeleton and details are noted around it (see p 35 of these notes).

> SHARED READING ACTIVITY

Language features and style

Return to the text and talk about how the language has been used to achieve the effects the author intended (see annotated example on p 34 of these notes).

Make particular reference to:

◆ the use of *connectives* to show contrast and progression;
◆ the degree of *formality* in the language used;
◆ the clear use of *paragraphs* to introduce a new aspect of Victorian society.

> INDEPENDENT ACTIVITY

Ask the pupils to take one of the aspects, e.g. a divided society, age of reforms, age of great changes, and to write up and present a one-minute talk. Use the report skeleton as a starting point but encourage the pupils to find extra information from other sources.

Writing a report text

Use pp 22–23 of *Victorian Children* pupils' book as a basis for the pupils' own report texts. You will need:

◆ the visual report on pp 22–23;
◆ p 32 of these notes enlarged/photocopied/made into an OHT for annotation.

Content and organization

SHARED READING ACTIVITY

Revise the content and organization of the report text from the previous session (see p 35 of these notes).

In pairs, pupils read and discuss the visual report on pp 22–23 of the pupils' book and make skeleton notes (see below). Notes should include content of the pages, details from the pictures, and any further information they may know. Their notes should be led by the following considerations: *What types of housing were available to the poor? (slums, tenement flats, back-to-back houses, basic cottages, workshops, workhouses). What were the conditions like? (dirty, disease-ridden, open sewers, contaminated waste, overcrowding).*

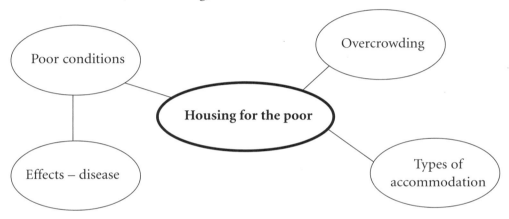

Language features and style

INDEPENDENT/ PAIRED READING AND WRITING ACTIVITY

Remind pupils of the language features and style of report texts (see p 32 of these notes).

Audience and purpose

Discuss the audience for pupils' reports (pupils who may/may not have preconceived ideas and expectations of Victorian life) and the purpose (to describe the appalling living conditions of the poor during Victorian times, and to emphasize the gulf between the rich and the poor during this era, i.e. in contrast to pp 14–15 of the pupils' book).

SHARED WRITING ACTIVITY

Demonstrate how to write a short introductory paragraph, for example:

Living conditions for the poor during Victorian times made for a cruel and unhealthy life for many. At best, a back-to-back house or a tenement flat would have been home to a large family. For the very poorest, the prison-like world of the workhouse would have been their home.

Each aspect of housing (as noted in the above report skeleton) needs its own paragraph. The first (after the introduction) might begin like this:

Proper sanitation, or the lack of it, became a major problem for the poor. Open sewers brought sewage flowing down the same streets in which local people bought and sold their food ...

INDEPENDENT WRITING ACTIVITY

Pupils should attempt to write similar paragraphs independently.

About report text

Audience and purpose

Audience – someone who wants to know about the topic.

Purpose – to describe what something is like.

Sometimes you may know more about the age or interests of your reader

Content and organization

- **non-chronological** information
- **introductory sentence or paragraph** says what the report is going to be about
- the information is sorted into groups or **categories**
- reports may include short pieces of explanation

This means it ISN'T written in time order, like a story or recount

What something looks like, where it is found . . .

Language features

- written in the **present tense**
- usually **general nouns and pronouns** (not particular people or things)
- **factual descriptive words**, not like the descriptions in a story
- words and devices that show **comparison and contrast**
- **third person** writing to make the report **impersonal and formal**
- **technical words and phrases** –which you may need to explain to the reader
- use of **examples** to help the reader understand the technical words

You would write about dogs in general, not a particular dog

You would say powerful beams, not beautiful bright beams

Expressions like have in common, the same as . . ., on the other hand, however. . .

Unusual words that go with the topic such as canine, translucent and wing span

Wingspan is the distance between the tips of a bird's outstretched wings

The basic skeleton for making notes is a spidergram

An example of a report text
Who were the Victorians?

Queen Victoria came to the throne in 1837. She was only 18 years old. She reigned for over 63 years – longer than any other British king or queen.

The growing empire

During Queen Victoria's reign, Britain became the most powerful nation in the world. Britain's empire grew to an enormous size. It stretched from Canada to New Zealand, and covered an amazing fifth of the world. Britain became very rich through the goods that poured in from all the countries in the empire. Wealth also increased through the growth of industry.

A divided society

This 'growth of industry' and the many technological changes helped throughout the era to create a society of three groups of people: the upper class, the middle class and the working class. The working class tended to work long hours in dirty and dangerous jobs to create wealth for the upper and middle classes. Even very young children had to work to help their families survive. The middle class increased as many more people owned businesses, or worked as managers or professionals. Middle class fathers earned enough money to buy a home, and their wives and children did not have to work. They were even able to employ servants.

Wages differed enormously. Poor children working in factories might earn £10 for a year's labour. An engineer could earn about £110 per year and a professional man, such as a senior civil servant, might earn around £700.

An age of reforms

A series of Reform Acts introduced during the Victorian era attempted to improve the lives of the poor, stopping very young children from working in mines and factories. Free schooling was introduced for everyone. Health reforms also attempted to make life better, by providing cleaner water, sewers and hospitals for even the poorest people.

Language features and style of the report text

Who were the Victorians?

Bold statement to introduce the topic

Queen Victoria came to the throne in 1837. She was only 18 years old. She reigned for over 63 years – longer than any other British king or queen.

A concise account of Victoria's reign – brief and factual

The growing empire

Key word (read around it and the next sentence to help define it)

During Queen Victoria's reign, Britain became the most powerful nation in the world. Britain's empire grew to an enormous size. It stretched from Canada to New Zealand, and covered an amazing fifth of the world. Britain became very rich through the goods that poured in from all the countries in the empire. Wealth also increased through the growth of industry.

A divided society

This 'growth of industry' and the many technological changes helped throughout the era to create a society of three groups of people: the upper class, the middle class and the working class. The working class tended to work long hours in dirty and dangerous jobs to create wealth for the upper and middle classes. Even very young children had to work to help their families survive. The middle class increased as many more people owned businesses, or worked as managers or professionals. Middle class fathers earned enough money to buy a home, and their wives and children did not have to work. They were even able to employ servants.

Opening sentence links with final sentence of previous paragraph – for continuity and progression

A good example of a complex sentence, using a conjunction (and), a connective to show example (such), and commas

Wages differed enormously. Poor children working in factories might earn £10 for a year's labour. An engineer could earn about £110 per year and a professional man, such as a senior civil servant, might earn around £700.

An age of reforms

A series of Reform Acts introduced during the Victorian era attempted to improve the lives of the poor, stopping very young children from working in mines and factories. Free schooling was introduced for everyone. Health reforms also attempted to make life better, by providing cleaner water, sewers and hospitals for even the poorest people.

Repetition of key word in a sentence which helps clarify its meaning, i.e. 'to make life better'

If you are using this text with other year groups then also highlight these features:

Y3/P4
- To become aware of the use of commas in marking grammatical boundaries within sentences (e.g. **During Queen Victoria's reign, Britain became the most powerful nation in the world**).
- Using pronouns to avoid repetition of proper nouns (e.g. **She reigned for over 63 years . . .**)

Y4/P5
- Identifying common adverbs with -ly suffix and discussing the impact they may have on the meaning in a sentence (e.g. **Wages differed enormously**).

Y6/P7
- To practise using hyphens to link clauses in a complex sentence (e.g. **She reigned for over sixty years – longer than any other British king or queen**).

Content and organization of the report text

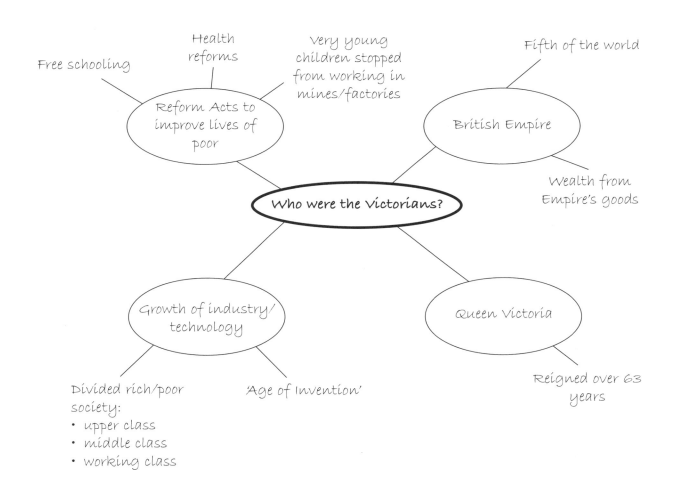

Teaching pupils how to read and write explanation text

Reading an explanation text

Page 38	Page 39
○→☼→↻	○→☼→↻
visual explanation	written explanation

Read pp 38–39 of *Victorian Children* pupils' book with the pupils. You will need:

◆ the written explanation on pp 38–39 (the text-only version on p 39 of these notes can be enlarged/photocopied/made into an OHT for annotation;

◆ p 38 of these notes enlarged/photocopied/made into an OHT for annotation.

Audience and purpose

> SHARED READING ACTIVITY

Talk about how the intended audience and purpose affects the language and layout of the text.

Audience – pupils in Year 5 who may have little or no knowledge of Victorian life and the technological advances that were made during this era.

Purpose – to report the main technological advances in communication that occurred during the Victorian period and to explain, in simple terms, how telegraph and telephone systems function.

Content and organization

> SHARED WRITING ACTIVITY

Demonstrate to the pupils how the content of this explanation text is organized by showing it (or parts of it) as an explanation skeleton (see p 41 of these notes).

Language features and style

> SHARED READING ACTIVITY

Return to the text and talk about the way language has been used to achieve the effects the author intended (see annotated example on p 40 of these notes).

Notice how the explanation text follows a set formula:
◆ *introducing* a new invention;
◆ *explaining the need and purpose* for the invention;
◆ *giving an explanatory sequence* of how it works.

> INDEPENDENT WRITING ACTIVITY

Using the explanation skeleton, ask the pupils to work in groups to create newspaper reports about the invention of the telegraph. Encourage the pupils to add pictures.

Writing an explanation text

Use p 36 of *Victorian Children* pupils' book as a basis for the pupils' own explanation texts. You will need:

◆ the visual explanation on p 36;
◆ p 38 of these notes enlarged/photocopied/made into an OHT for annotation.

SHARED
READING
ACTIVITY

Content and organization

Revise the content and organization of the explanation text from the previous session.

Pairs of pupils discuss the visual explanation on p 36 of the pupils' book and make skeleton notes. Their notes should be guided by the following questions:
Why is coal used? How is the water heated? What happens to the steam? What forces the pistons to move?

INDEPENDENT/
PAIRED READING
AND WRITING
ACTIVITY

Language features and style

Remind pupils of the language features of explanation texts (see p 38 of these notes).

Audience and purpose

Discuss the audience for the pupils' explanation texts (readers who know little or nothing about how a steam locomotive is powered) and the purpose (to give basic information about how a steam locomotive is powered).

SHARED
WRITING
ACTIVITY

Discuss with the pupils the task of turning the visual explanation of the steam locomotive into a written explanation.

Demonstrate how to write an introductory paragraph, e.g.

A steam locomotive relies upon coal-fired boilers for its source of power. Water is heated over the burning coal in a boiler. As the water boils, it turns to steam – which is then fed into cylinders containing pistons. As the steam expands inside the cylinders, the pistons are forced backwards and forwards . . .

INDEPENDENT
WRITING
ACTIVITY

Ask pupils to write up the remaining paragraphs independently.

About explanation text

Audience and purpose

Audience – someone who wants to understand the process (how or why it happens).

Purpose – to explain how or why something happens.

> Sometimes you may know more about the age or interests of your reader

Content and organization

- **title** often asks a question, or says clearly what the explanation is about
- text often opens with **general statement(s)** to introduce important words or ideas
- the process is then written in a **series of logical steps**, usually in **time order**
- sometimes **picture(s) or diagram(s)**

> This happens... then this happens... next...

Language features

- **third person** writing to make the explanation **impersonal and formal**
- written in the **present tense**
- usually **general nouns and pronouns** (not particular people or things)
- **factual descriptive words,** not like the descriptions in a story
- **technical words and phrases** – which you may need to explain to the reader
- words and devices that show **sequence**
- words and devices that show **cause and effect**

> You would say *powerful beams,* not *beautiful bright beams*

> You would write about dogs in general, not a particular dog

> Unusual words that go with the topic such as *canine, translucent* and *wingspan*

> First..., next..., finally

> If..., then... This happens because... This means that...

The basic skeleton for making notes is a flowchart

> The explanation skeleton can change depending on the sort of process

An example of an explanation text

International communications

As the British Empire grew so did the need to communicate with the many colonies around the world. Letters would often take weeks before they reached their destinations, even when carried by the new steamships.

In 1937, the telegraph was invented and this helped to send messages faster across greater distances. The telegraph works by using electricity to send messages along wires. The messages were transmitted using Morse Code, invented by Samuel Morse in 1843. This was a system of dots and dashes tapped out at one end of the wire and then heard at the other end of the wire. The series of dots and dashes was a code, representing the different letters of the alphabet. The person receiving the telegraph message had to decipher the code into letters and words.

However, it wasn't until the first transatlantic telegraph cable was laid successfully between Britain and America in 1866 that the modern era of international communications really began.

Alexander Graham Bell was experimenting with a telegraph machine, sending more than one message at a time. As a result of his experiments, he began to work out how to transmit sounds and then developed the telephone. The telephone allowed people to actually speak to one another.

After the success of his invention, Bell also invented the telephone exchange as the demand for telephones increased. Telephone exchanges allowed several calls to happen at once. The first exchange in Britain was built in the 1870s but telephones did not become widespread until after the Victorian era.

Language features and style of the explanation text

Concise title to define the subject to be explained

International communications

Key words explained in glossary

As the British Empire grew so did the need to communicate with the many colonies around the world. Letters would often take weeks before they reached their destinations, even when carried by the new steamships.

Technical vocabulary, followed by origins of name and sequential explanation of function/ purpose

In 1937, the telegraph was invented and this helped to send messages faster across greater distances. The telegraph works by using electricity to send messages along wires. The messages were transmitted using Morse Code, invented by Samuel Morse in 1843. This was a system of dots and dashes tapped out at one end of the wire and then heard at the other end of the wire. The series of dots and dashes was a code, representing the different letters of the alphabet. The person receiving the telegraph message had to decipher the code into letters and words.

Words showing cause and effect

However, it wasn't until the first transatlantic telegraph cable was laid successfully between Britain and America in 1866 that the modern era of international communications really began.

Link with title

Alexander Graham Bell was experimenting with a telegraph machine, sending more than one message at a time. As a result of his experiments, he began to work out how to transmit sounds and then developed the telephone. The telephone allowed people to actually speak to one another.

Adverbial clause showing reason and progression

Preposition to show time and give chronological structure

After the success of his invention, Bell also invented the telephone exchange as the demand for telephones increased. Telephone exchanges allowed several calls to happen at once. The first exchange in Britain was built in the 1870s but telephones did not become widespread until after the Victorian era.

If you are using this text with other year groups then also highlight these features:

Y3/P4
- ◆ Summarizing the content of a paragraph orally.
- ◆ Developing note-taking skills – pupils to make their own notes on each invention.

Y4/P5
- ◆ Identifying different types of text by looking at structure, content, vocabulary, layout, style, and purpose.

Y6/P7
- ◆ Using clauses and phrases to show cause and effect (e.g. **As a result . . .**).

Content and organization of the explanation text

International communications

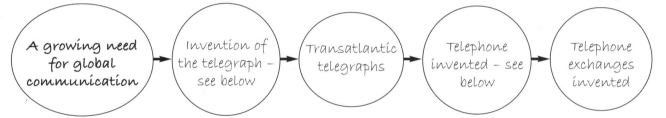

How does a telegraph work?

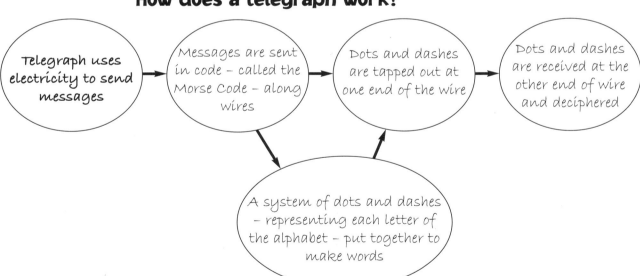

How does a telephone work?

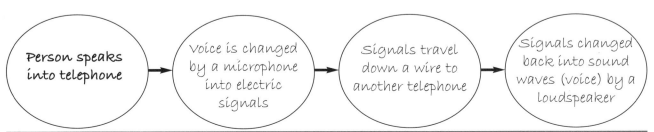

Teaching pupils how to read and write persuasion text

Reading persuasion text

Page 27
written persuasion

Read p 27 of *Victorian Children* pupils' book with the pupils. You will need:

- ◆ the written persuasion (letter) on p 27 (the text-only version on p 45 of these notes can be enlarged/photocopied/made into an OHT for annotation);
- ◆ p 44 of these notes enlarged/photocopied/made into an OHT for annotation.

> SHARED READING ACTIVITY

Audience and purpose

Talk about how the intended audience and purpose affects language and layout.

Audience – readers of the newspaper, who are opposed to the programme of public spending on sanitation systems.

Purpose – to persuade them that unless money is spent on proper drainage and water systems in London, cholera will continue to spread and many lives will be lost.

> SHARED WRITING ACTIVITY

Content and organization

Demonstrate to the pupils how the content of this persuasive letter is organized by showing it as a persuasion skeleton (see p 47 of these notes).

> SHARED READING ACTIVITY

Language features and style

Return to the text and talk about the way language has been used to achieve the effects the writer intended (see annotated example on p 46 of these notes).

> INDEPENDENT ACTIVITY

Ask the pupils to use the persuasion skeleton to help them present the letter as a *propaganda poster* (see p 47 of these notes), showing the awful effects of poor sanitation and the need to act now to prevent the spread of disease.

Writing a persuasion text

Use p 31 of *Victorian Children* pupils' book as a basis for the pupils' own persuasive texts. You will need:

◆ the visual persuasion on p 31;
◆ p 44 of these notes enlarged/photocopied/made into an OHT for annotation.

Content and organization

> SHARED
> READING
> ACTIVITY

Revise the content and organization of explanation text from the previous session (see p 47 of these notes). Focus particularly on the layout and style of the visual persuasion text (poster).

> INDEPENDENT/
> PAIRED READING
> AND WRITING
> ACTIVITY

Ask pairs of pupils to read and discuss the advertisement for *Benham's Ventilating Kitchener* on p 31 of the pupils' book.

Ask the pupils to imagine they have their own *Benham's Ventilating Kitchener*. They are delighted with it and decide to write a letter to a newspaper, recommending the product to its readers.

To prepare for this task, ask the pupils to make skeleton notes (bullet points) of what they want to say in the written text (letter). For example, begin like this:

◆ *introduce myself as a happy customer of Benham's and a user of their Ventilating Kitchener which I would like to recommend to readers;*
◆ *describe the advantages of this product (e.g. no brickwork required, easy to install in a few hours).*

Language features and style

> SHARED
> WRITING
> ACTIVITY

Remind pupils of the language features and style of persuasion texts (see p 44 of these notes).

Audience and purpose

Discuss the audience for pupils' letters (readers of the newspaper who may/may not have heard of *Benham's Ventilating Kitchener*) and the purpose (to persuade readers to purchase their own *Benham's Ventilating Kitchener*).

Demonstrate writing the opening paragraphs of the written persuasive text (letter), e.g.

Dear Sir,

As the proud owner of my very own Benham's Ventilating Kitchener, I should like to recommend the appliance to your readers.

When the local workmen arrived to install the Kitchener I feared that they would be here for some considerable time, pulling my kitchen apart to install the appliance properly. I was pleasantly surprised to find that the whole operation took just three hours and required no extra brickwork at all – brilliant!

> INDEPENDENT
> WRITING
> ACTIVITY

Ask the pupils to write their own letters as above.

About persuasion text

Audience and purpose

Audience – someone you want to persuade, but who may not know much about the subject.

Purpose – to argue the case for a point of view, persuade someone to buy something or support a cause.

Sometimes you may know more about the age or interests of your reader

Content and organization

◆ usually starts with a sentence or paragraph to **introduce the argument**
◆ the argument is then split into a number of **main points,** each of which probably needs some **elaboration**
◆ **concluding sentence or paragraph** sums up the argument

You may have to introduce some important words or ideas the reader needs to know

The elaboration could be
– reasons for agreeing with the point
– examples to back it up
– further information to explain it.

Language features

◆ writing may be personal (**first and second person**) or impersonal (**third person**)
◆ written in the **present tense**
◆ language may be quite **emotional**, more like a story than other non-fiction
◆ there may be **rhetorical questions,** which do not really expect an answer
◆ words and devices showing **cause and effect,** used to **argue** the case
◆ words and devices that show **movement from one point to the next**

Use powerful verbs and adjectives, exaggerations or repetition to make an effect

Is this really important?

Therefore..., Consequently..., This means that...

Firstly...., Another reason that..., Thirdly...

The basic skeleton for making notes is pronged bullet points

An example of persuasion text

Dear Sir

I am writing to inform those readers who are opposed to the programme of public spending on sanitation of the terrible health problems to be found in the middle of our city of London. I am writing to insist that they support the programme so that proper drains and clean water systems are provided.

I went to visit the Narrow Street area where a terrible outbreak of cholera had occurred. It is an area where the sewers are decaying and the cesspits are undrained. I have for some time believed that water full of germs spreads cholera from person to person. Here, cholera came from a single source of polluted water – the public water pump. I took a sample of the fetid water from the pump and looked at it under the microscope. It contained tiny white floating specks – the infection! I immediately went to the Board of Guardians of St John's Parish. I urged them to remove the pump handle to stop people from obtaining the infected water. They agreed and the spread of cholera dramatically dropped but not before 616 people had died.

Now that we know how cholera is spread, it is our duty to provide proper drains and an organized water system to banish the scourge of cholera from our streets forever.

Yours truly
Dr Snow
London

Language features and style of the persuasion text

Use of first person narrative – to show personal experience

Use of a strong verb – to persuade the reader to act

Strong anecdotal evidence to support the argument/ persuade the reader

A final emotional plea – use of the phrase 'it is our duty' is effective

First paragraph introduces the argument

Another strong verb to show the writer's determination and the need to act

Dear Sir

I am writing to inform those readers who are opposed to the programme of public spending on sanitation of the terrible health problems to be found in the middle of our city of London. I am writing to insist that they support the programme so that proper drains and clean water systems are provided.

I went to visit the Narrow Street area where a terrible outbreak of cholera had occurred. It is an area where the sewers are decaying and the cesspits are undrained. I have for some time believed that water full of germs spreads cholera from person to person. Here, cholera came from a single source of polluted water – the public water pump. I took a sample of the fetid water from the pump and looked at it under the microscope. It contained tiny white floating specks – the infection! I immediately went to the Board of Guardians of St John's Parish. I urged them to remove the pump handle to stop people from obtaining the infected water. They agreed and the spread of cholera dramatically dropped but not before 616 people had died.

Now that we know how cholera is spread, it is our duty to provide proper drains and an organized water system to banish the scourge of cholera from our streets forever.

Yours truly
Dr Snow
London

If you are using this text with other year groups then also highlight these features:

Y3/P4
◆ Identifying pronouns in sentences and recognising first person narrative (e.g. **I am writing to inform you** ...).

Y4/P5
◆ Understanding the effects of using powerful verbs in a sentence (e.g. **I am writing to insist that they support** ...).

Y6/P7
◆ Reporting on events in a journalistic style – pupils to pretend they are a journalist reporting on the plight of the residents of **Narrow Street**.

Content and organization of the persuasion text

The content and organisation of the persuasion text (letter) on p 27 can be shown in the following bullet points:

◆ introductory paragraph: to all readers opposed to the public spending on sanitation; to persuade them that unless we improve the drainage and water systems, many more people will die;

◆ give anecdotal evidence: talk about my visit to Narrow Street; introduce this area; explain how the sewers are decaying and the cesspits are not drained;

◆ show how water full of germs spreads disease from person to person; describe the water pump I found with fetid water, full of germs; explain how once it was replaced the cases of cholera dropped dramatically.

The content (argument) can also be presented in visual form, using a **poster**:

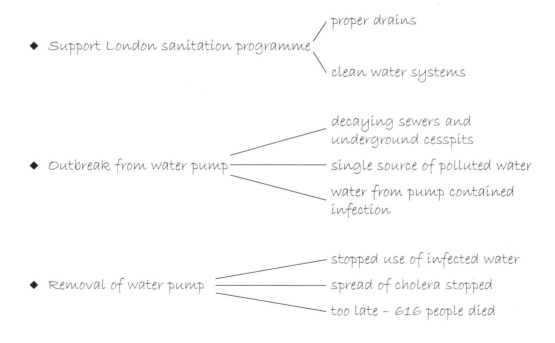

◆ Support London sanitation programme
  — proper drains
  — clean water systems

◆ Outbreak from water pump
  — decaying sewers and underground cesspits
  — single source of polluted water
  — water from pump contained infection

◆ Removal of water pump
  — stopped use of infected water
  — spread of cholera stopped
  — too late – 616 people died

Page	Contents	Text Type	National Literacy Strategy Objectives	QCA History Objectives Units 11 and 12
				Pupils should learn:
2	Concept map and Contents		T2 TL 17	
4	Who were the Victorians?	Written report Visual recount	T2 TL 16, 20, 22 T2 SL 5, 7, 9 T1 TL 21, 23, 24, 26, 27 T1 SL 1, 3, 5 T1 WL 2, 3	• to identify Queen Victoria and place the Victorian period in relation to other periods of British history • to consider what life was like for children in the past
6	Views of childhood	Written discussion Visual persuasion	T1 23, 26 T2 20, 21 T3 19	• to consider what life was like for children in the past • to collect information from a range of sources and draw conclusions about the Victorian period • to understand that ways of life differed greatly across Victorian society • to consider how attitudes to children and childhood changed over time
8	Life for the middle classes	Visual recount	T1 TL 21, 23, 24, 26, 27 T1 SL 1, 3, 5 T1 WL 2, 3	• to consider what life was like for children in the past • to consider how attitudes to children and childhood changed over time • to recall information about the life of children in Victorian times
10	Victorian games and toys	Written and visual instructions	T1 TL 22, 23, 26, 27 T1 SL 3, 4, 8, 9	
12	Clothes	Written report	T2 TL 20, 22, 23, 24 T2 SL 3, 5, 7, 9, 10 T2 WL 2, 3, 9	
14	Houses	Visual report	T2 TL 16, 20, 22 T2 SL 5, 7, 9	• to understand that ways of life differed greatly across Victorian society
16	Schools	Written report	T2 TL 16, 20, 22, 23, 24 T2 SL 3, 5, 7, 9, 10 T2 WL 2, 3, 9	• to consider what life was like for children in the past to compare modern and Victorian schooling
18	Life of the poor – a journal	Written recount	T1 TL 21, 23, 24, 26, 27 T1 SL 1, 3, 4, 5, 8	• to consider what life was like for children in the past to • understand that ways of life differed greatly across Victorian society • to recall information about the life of children in Victorian times
20	Children at work	Visual discussion	T2 TL 16, 20, 22 T2 SL 5, 7, 9	• to consider what life was like for children in the past • to consider how attitudes to children and childhood changed over time
22	Housing for the poor	Visual report	T2 TL 20, 22, 23, 24 T2 SL 3, 5, 7, 9, 10 T2 WL 2, 3, 9	• to understand that ways of life differed greatly across Victorian society
24	The Victorian underworld	Written report	T2 TL 16, 20, 22 T2 SL 5, 7, 9	• to understand that ways of life differed greatly across Victorian society
26	Unhealthy Britain	Written explanation Written persuasion	T2 TL 15, 16, 19, 21 T2 SL 8, 9 T2 WL 9 T3 TL 12, 14, 15, 16, 17, 19 T3 SL 4, 6, 7	
28	Who improved the lives of the poor?	Written and visual recount	T1 TL 21, 23, 24, 26, 27 T1 SL 1, 3, 4, 5, 8 T1 WL 2, 3	• to understand that the work of individuals can change aspects of society • to find out about important figures in Victorian times
30	Victorian food and shopping	Written report Visual persuasion	T2 TL 16, 20, 22 T2 SL 5, 7, 9	• to collect information from a range of sources and draw conclusions about the Victorian period
32	Victorian recipes	Written and visual instructions	T1 TL 22, 23, 26, 27 T1 SL 3, 4, 8, 9	
34	The railway experience	Written persuasion Written recount	T1 TL 21, 23, 24, 26, 27 T1 SL 1, 3, 4, 5, 8 T1 WL 2, 3	• to describe the attitudes of some different people to the building of a railway in the locality • to communicate their understanding of benefits and disadvantages of railways
36	Railway developments	Visual explanation Visual recount	T1 21, 23, 24, 26 T2 21, 22	
38	Technological advances	Written and visual explanation Written report	T2 TL 16, 20, 22 T2 SL 5, 7, 9 T2 TL 15, 16, 19, 21 T2 SL 8, 9 T2 WL 9	• to collect information from a range of sources and draw conclusions about the Victorian period
40	Leisure time	Visual Report	T2 TL 20, 22, 23, 24 T2 SL 3, 5, 7, 9, 10 T2 WL 2, 3, 9	• to collect information from a range of sources and draw conclusions about the Victorian period
42	The Empire	Written and visual report Visual discussion	T2 TL 16, 20, 22 T2 SL 5, 7, 9	• to collect information from a range of sources and draw conclusions about the Victorian period
44	Victorian legacies	Written and visual report	T2 TL 20, 22, 23, 24 T2 SL 3, 5, 7, 9, 10 T2 WL 2, 3, 9	• to collect information from a range of sources and draw conclusions about the Victorian period